Freed-Up IN LATER LIFE

Planning Now for Beyond 65

Freed-Up in Later Life

Planning Now for Beyond 65

PARTICIPANT'S WORKBOOK

DICK TOWNER

Freed-Up in Later Life Participant's Workbook
Copyright © 2009 by Willow Creek Association

Requests for information should be addressed to:
Willow Creek Association
67 E. Algonquin Road
South Barrington, IL 60010

ISBN: 0744198585

All Scripture quotations are taken from New Revised Standard Version Bible, copyright
1989, Division of Christian Education of the National Council of the Churches of Christ in
the United States of America. Used by permission. All rights reserved.

All rights reserved. No part of this publication may be reproduced, stored in a retrieval
system, or transmitted in any form or by any means – electronic, mechanical, photocopy,
recording, or any other – except for brief quotations in printed reviews, without the prior
permission of the publisher.

Cover and interior design by Daab Creative

Printed in the United States of America

09 10 11 12 13 14 15 • 10 9 8 7 6 5 4 3 2 1

Contents

Foreword 08

Acknowledgements 09

Session 1 10

Session 2 38

Notes 59

FACILITATOR'S NOTE: This course can be used by individuals, in a small group or presented as a workshop. In the latter two cases it is helpful to have a Facilitator. A free Facilitator's Guide can be found at www.goodsenseministry.com. Go to the RESOURCES link and download the *Freed-Up in Later Life Facilitator's Guide*.

Foreword

Retirement is a popular topic of conversation these days for understandable reasons. It's 2009 and the oldest of the Baby Boomers are becoming eligible for Social Security. We're in an economic quagmire and no one is quite sure what the solution is or how long it will take to right the ship. The validity of some of our assumptions about "life after 65" is being challenged. It's a great time to take a hard look at retirement — or, better yet, let's call it "later life."

This workshop looks at planning for later life from a biblical perspective, explores some of the common assumptions about retirement, points out how to best prepare financially for later life and covers the basics of long-term investing. It provides a wealth of information and places it in a biblical context.

Regardless of where you are in life's journey, I hope this workshop will be informative and remove anxiety about an often misunderstood time of life.

Sincerely in Christ,
Dick Towner

Acknowledgements

Few things in life can be accomplished alone and that is certainly true for this resource. To use a phrase from a popular song, "We all need each other." So for their professional expertise, but even more so for their spirit of unselfish helpfulness, I deeply thank the following colleagues and friends:

Erica Dekker
Tim Giardino
Bob Gustafson
Pete Kosmal
Dan Kotter
Lucas Mroz
Stephanie Oakley
Dave Olson
Chris Scherf
Sarah Trommer

SESSION 1

What Does Retirement Mean?

- The Bible doesn't say anything about "retirement" as we've come to conceive of it.

- The dictionary defines the word "retire" as "to depart for rest; to remove oneself from the daily routine of working."[1]

Activity

Take a moment and write down your definition of retirement. Then, turn to one or two others and share that definition.

Financial Implications

- How we would like to live during our later years has pronounced financial implications.

- Money is a big deal to us — and to God.

History of Retirement

- Retirement is a recently developed form of social engineering.

- Society used to be family centered — children supported older family members until death.

- After the Great Depression, the government introduced Social Security for persons aged 65[2] — though at the time, life expectancy in the U.S. was 63.

- The intent of Social Security was to encourage older workers to leave the workforce and open jobs for younger workers.

- Retirement has been portrayed as a lifestyle of leisure to which citizens have a right as of age 65 (if not before).[3]

Misperceptions about Retirement

- Misperception #1: Age 65 is old, signaling a brief time of declining health until death.

  - » Today, life expectancy for those who reach 65 is into the 80s.[4]

  - » Financial advisors suggest assuming you may live into your 90s.

- Misperception #2: Leisure is just as fulfilling as meaningful work.

  - » Two-thirds of people say they plan to work for pay after they retire because they enjoy working and want to stay involved.[5]

  - » Retirement without meaningful involvement or contribution to others leads to high rates of depression, illness, and not infrequently, death.[6]

- Misperception #3: Older workers should make room for younger ones.

  » The current Social Security system was designed when massive numbers of younger workers needed jobs.[7]

  » The experience of the older worker can be a huge asset.

- Misperception #4: People over 65 are less productive.

  » The elderly make fewer mistakes and have fewer accidents, lower absenteeism, and, in all but the most physically demanding work, higher productivity.[8]

Activity

These are very common misperceptions. Which one of them resonates most with you? Take a few moments to share with those around you.

- ❏ *Age 65 is old.*
- ❏ *Leisure is just as fulfilling as meaningful work.*
- ❏ *Older workers should make room for younger ones.*
- ❏ *People over 65 are less productive.*

Later Life

A New Perspective

- God's plan is that all the days of our life have meaning and purpose beyond ourselves.

- The key question is not "When will I be able to retire?" but "What do I want my later years to look like?"

- It's about values and purpose, not money and leisure.

Key Areas to Consider

- Key Area #1: Priorities
  What will be most important to you?

- Key Area #2: Lifestyle
  What lifestyle do you want to have?
  How will it be different from your present lifestyle?

- Key Area #3: Work
  Will you continue working as-is?
  Continue working but on your own terms?
  Work in a different capacity you've always thought about?
  Regularly volunteer?

- Key Area #4: Housing
  What will be your living arrangement — house, apartment,
  condo, travel home, retirement community?

- Key Area #5: Location
  Where will you live geographically — same locale, different
  part of the country, near your children?
  If a different location, what is the cost of living there?

- Key Area #6: Income
  What will be your sources of income?

Activity

Take a few moments to look at the questions below and jot down some initial thoughts — whatever comes to mind.

What are your most important priorities?

What lifestyle do you want to have?

Will you work? In what fashion?

What type of living arrangement will you have?

Where will you live geographically?

What will be your source of income?

Enough

- Planning for later life raises some financial questions, such as:

  » How much money is enough?

  » How do I get enough?

  » How will I know it's enough?

- Answering questions about "enough" raises still other questions:

  » How much will inflation be?

  » How much will my investments return?

  » How healthy will I be?

  » How long will I live?

- For planning purposes, make conservative assumptions, such as:

  » An inflation rate that is at least the historic average.

  » Investment returns that are less than what some might say is OK to assume.

  » That you'll live to be a ripe old age.

Five Ways to Prepare Financially

1) Begin Now to be Prudent in Your Spending

- A prudent spender is one who:

  » Enjoys the fruits of their labor yet guards against materialism.

  » Lives within their means.

  » Understands the difference between needs and wants.

  » Leads a lifestyle marked by discipline, moderation, and the learned mindset of contentment.

2) Have a Budget and Keep Records

- A budget is a spending plan that diverts money to where it needs to go.

- A budget is not restrictive but freedom producing.

3) Have a Debt Elimination Plan

- Get out of consumer debt (debt on anything that is depreciating in value) as quickly as possible.

- The borrower really is slave to the lender (Proverbs 22:7).

- Paying off your mortgage before later life is also a goal to pursue.

4) Be a Generous Giver

- There is a significant amount of biblical evidence that God will honor a generous spirit.

- Giving is key to overall control of our money.

- There is a unique joy that comes from being generous.

5) Be a Wise Saver in the Long and Short Term

- You need short-term, readily available savings to deal with the unexpected, in addition to long-term savings for later life.

- A key to long-term savings is saving on a regular basis.

- With a long timeframe and the power of compounding, the amount need not be great.

- If you don't have a long timeframe, future circumstances (e.g. grown children, house paid for) may allow significantly larger contributions to be made in the remaining years.

Activity

Which of these five things do you feel might be hardest for you? Make a check next to it below, and if you want to, write down one action step you might take in that area.

- ❏ *Begin now to be prudent in your spending.*
- ❏ *Have a budget and keep records.*
- ❏ *Have a debt elimination plan.*
- ❏ *Be a generous giver.*
- ❏ *Be a wise saver in the long and short term.*

Action step:

SESSION **ONE** 23

Ballpark E$timate®

About the Ballpark E$timate

The Ballpark E$timate® offers a way to obtain a rough first estimate of what you will need for retirement. The annual amount it suggests you save reflects today's dollars; therefore, you will need to recalculate your retirement needs annually and as your salary and circumstances change.

The tool assumes investments will earn 3 percent above inflation, wages will grow at the same rate as inflation, and you will begin to receive Social Security benefits at age 65.

© Copyright, EBRI Education and Research Fund. All rights reserved. Used by permission.

Example

Joe Jones is 35 years old and currently makes $45,000 a year. Mary Jones is also 35 and works part-time making $20,000, for a combined total of $65,000. Both plan to retire at age 65, although Joe plans to earn $6,000 per year from part-time work. They have $31,670 already saved.

1) How much annual income will you want in retirement?

($45,000 + $20,000) x .85 = **$55,000**

- Figure at least 70 percent of your current annual gross income just to maintain your current standard of living.

- Use 70–80 percent if: You will need to pay for the basics in retirement, but you won't have to pay many medical expenses as your employer pays the Medicare Part B and D premium and provides employer-paid retiree health insurance. You're planning for a comfortable retirement without much travel. You are older and/or in your prime earning years.

- Use 80–90 percent if: You will need to pay your Medicare Part B and D premiums and pay for insurance to cover medical costs above Medicare, which on average covers about 55 percent. You plan to take some small trips, and you know you will need to continue saving some money.

- Use 100–120 percent if: You will need to cover all Medicare and other health care costs. You are very young and/or your prime earning years are ahead of you. You would like a retirement lifestyle that is more than comfortable. You need to save for the possibility of long-term care.

2) Subtract the income you expect to receive annually from:

Social Security

$14,500 + $8,000 =   **- $22,500**

If you make under $25,000, enter $8,000; between $25,000-$40,000, enter $12,000; over $40,000, enter $14,500. (For married couples, the lower earning spouse should enter either their own benefit based on their income or 50 percent of the higher earning spouse's benefit, whichever is higher.)

Traditional Employer Pension   -$0

A plan that pays a set dollar amount for life, where the dollar amount depends on salary and years of service (in today's dollars) — not a 401(k), IRA, etc.

Part-time income   -$6,000

Other   -$0

Reverse annuity mortgage payments, earnings on assets, etc.

> **This is how much you need to make up for each retirement year:**
> $55,000 - $22,500 - $6,000 = **$26,500**

3) To determine the amount you'll need to save, multiply the amount you need to make up by a factor based on gender and life expectancy.

$26,500 x 18.79 = **$497,935**

- Look at the chart on the next page for your gender. For married couples, choose the female for the most conservative result.

- Find the age you plan to retire.

- Make an assumption of your life expectancy. (Choose a higher age for a more conservative estimate.)

MALE

Age you expect to retire	Life Expectancy		
	Age 82 50th percentile	Age 89 75th percentile	Age 94 90th percentile
55	18.79	21.71	23.46
60	16.31	19.68	21.71
65	13.45	17.35	19.68
70	10.15	14.65	17.35

FEMALE

Age you expect to retire	Life Expectancy		
	Age 86 50th percentile	Age 92 75th percentile	Age 97 90th percentile
55	20.53	22.79	24.40
60	18.32	20.93	22.79
65	15.77	18.79	20.93
70	12.83	16.31	18.79

4) If you expect to retire before age 65, multiply your Social Security benefit from step 2 by the factor below. + $0

Expect to retire at 55 ▸ 8.8   Expect to retire at 60 ▸ 4.7

5) Multiply your savings to date by the factor below (include money accumulated in a 401(k), IRA, or similar retirement plan).

$31,670 x 2.4 =   **-$76,008**

If you plan to retire in:

10 years ▶ 1.3	30 years ▶ 2.4
15 years ▶ 1.6	35 years ▶ 2.8
20 years ▶ 1.8	40 years ▶ 3.3
25 years ▶ 2.1	

Total additional savings needed at retirement:
$497,935 + 0 - $76,008 =   **$421,927**

6) To determine the ANNUAL amount you'll need to save, multiply the TOTAL amount by the factor below.

$421,927 x .020 =   **$8,439**

If you plan to retire in:

10 years ▸ .085   30 years ▸ .020
15 years ▸ .052   35 years ▸ .016
20 years ▸ .036   40 years ▸ .013

Monthly amount you need to save:
$8,439 ÷ 12 =   **$703**

Your Ballpark E$timate®

1) How much annual income will you want in retirement? $_____

- Figure at least 70 percent of your current annual gross income just to maintain your current standard of living.

- Use 70–80 percent if: You will need to pay for the basics in retirement, but you won't have to pay many medical expenses as your employer pays the Medicare Part B and D premium and provides employer-paid retiree health insurance. You're planning for a comfortable retirement without much travel. You are older and/or in your prime earning years.

- Use 80–90 percent if: You will need to pay your Medicare Part B and D premiums and pay for insurance to cover medical costs above Medicare, which on average covers about 55 percent. You plan to take some small trips, and you know you will need to continue saving some money.

- Use 100–120 percent if: You will need to cover all Medicare and other health care costs. You are very young and/or your prime earning years are ahead of you. You would like a retirement lifestyle that is more than comfortable. You need to save for the possibility of long-term care.

2) Subtract the income you expect to receive annually from:

Social Security   -$ _____

If you make under $25,000, enter $8,000; between $25,000–$40,000, enter $12,000; over $40,000, enter $14,500. (For married couples, the lower earning spouse should enter either their own benefit based on their income or 50 percent of the higher earning spouse's benefit, whichever is higher.)

Traditional Employer Pension   -$ _____

A plan that pays a set dollar amount for life, where the dollar amount depends on salary and years of service (in today's dollars)

Part-time income   -$ _____

Other   -$ _____

Reverse annuity mortgage payments, earnings on assets, etc.

> **This is how much you need to make up for each retirement year:**
> = $ _____

3) To determine the amount you'll need to save, multiply the amount you need to make up by a factor based on gender and life expectancy.

$ _____

- Look at the chart on the next page for your gender. For married couples, choose the female for the most conservative result.

- Find the age you plan to retire.

- Make an assumption of your life expectancy. (Choose a higher age for a more conservative estimate.)

SESSION **ONE** 33

MALE

	Life Expectancy		
Age you expect to retire	Age 82 50th percentile	Age 89 75th percentile	Age 94 90th percentile
55	18.79	21.71	23.46
60	16.31	19.68	21.71
65	13.45	17.35	19.68
70	10.15	14.65	17.35

FEMALE

	Life Expectancy		
Age you expect to retire	Age 86 50th percentile	Age 92 75th percentile	Age 97 90th percentile
55	20.53	22.79	24.40
60	18.32	20.93	22.79
65	15.77	18.79	20.93
70	12.83	16.31	18.79

4) If you expect to retire before age 65, multiply your Social Security benefit from step 2 by the factor below.

+ $_____

Expect to retire at 55 ▸ 8.8   Expect to retire at 60 ▸ 4.7

5) Multiply your savings to date by the factor below (include money accumulated in a 401(k), IRA, or similar retirement plan).

- $ _____

If you plan to retire in:

10 years ▸ 1.3	30 years ▸ 2.4
15 years ▸ 1.6	35 years ▸ 2.8
20 years ▸ 1.8	40 years ▸ 3.3
25 years ▸ 2.1	

Total additional savings needed at retirement:
= $ _____

6) To determine the ANNUAL amount you'll need to save, multiply the TOTAL amount by the factor below.

$ _____

If you plan to retire in:

10 years ▸ .085	30 years ▸ .020
15 years ▸ .052	35 years ▸ .016
20 years ▸ .036	40 years ▸ .013
25 years ▸ .027	

Monthly amount you'll need to save:
ANNUAL amount ÷ 12 = $ _____

What's Next

- If the amount you need to save seems overwhelming, don't be discouraged!

  » Working a bit longer before retirement or a small amount of after-retirement income can significantly lower the amount that needs to be saved.

  » Visit **www.choosetosave.org/ballpark** for an interactive version of the Ballpark E$timate® with more assumptions that you can change.

  » Begin now, follow the principles, and do the best you can under existing circumstances.

- If you find that reaching your goal will be fairly easy, way to go!

  » Be sure you've answered the question, "When is enough, enough?"

  » Be careful not to find yourself in the position of simply saving more just to save more — "building bigger barns" (Luke 12:13-21).

SESSION **ONE** 37

SESSION 2

Investing

> **Investing**
> Putting money into commercial undertakings (e.g. business, real estate, stocks, bonds) subject to modest levels of risk, expecting a reasonable rate of return over a long period of time.

Two Basic Ways to Invest Your Money

- 1) Lend it at an agreed-upon interest rate.
  Examples: Putting money in a savings account or CD, buying a bond

- 2) Become a part owner.
  Examples: Buying stocks, shares of mutual funds, real estate, or other hard assets

Risk and Return

- There is always a relationship between risk and return.

  - » The greater the potential return, the greater the potential risk.

  - » High-risk investments have a greater potential for higher returns, but they will not always produce higher returns.

  - » Low-risk investments will seldom yield high returns.

- Owning generally involves more risk than lending.

  - » Lending is at a set interest rate to an institution like a bank, which is insured by the FDIC, so it has very little risk.

  - » In contrast, when you become a part owner, you do not know the return you will receive, but that greater risk means higher potential gain.

Risk Tolerance

> **Risk Tolerance**
> The level of risk you are comfortable taking with your investments.

- Your risk tolerance has to do with your temperament and background.

- Your risk tolerance determines which investment options are best for you.

- Consider how comfortable you are with big swings in value in the short term.

- If you violate your risk tolerance, besides creating undue personal stress, you will react emotionally when setbacks occur.

Online Risk Tolerance Tests

https://personal.vanguard.com/us/ FundsInvQuestionnaire

www.tiaa-cref.org/calcs/allocation
(Simpler to use, but does not take as many personal factors into consideration)

http://helpmefinancial.com/calculators
(Look under "Investment Calculators" for "What is my risk tolerance?" The results page lists related calculators and helpful articles.)

Note: These tests are provided for informational purposes, and the investment companies and their funds are not endorsed by the author or publishers.

Activity

Given what we've just talked about and the results of your Ballpark E$timate®, read the statements below and pick the one that best describes you, and then share your answer with one or two other people.

❑ *As long as my investments are likely to grow in the long term, I'm fine with short-term drops.*

❑ *I can handle a few small drops for the sake of higher returns, but not many.*

❑ *I'm more interested in minimizing the risk of even short-term drops than maximizing returns.*

Responsibility

> **Socially Responsible Investing**
> Considering how the money you are investing will be used.

- A growing number of mutual funds have been established that screen out stocks based on a variety of socially responsible criteria.

- Examples of Socially Responsible Funds
  Note: These funds are provided for informational purposes and are not endorsed by the author or publishers.

  » Ariel

  » Calvert

  » Domini

  » MMA Praxis

  » Pax World

  » Winslow

- Visit **www.socialinvest.org/resources/pubs** for more information on this type of investing.

Determining What to Invest In

Historical Returns

Compound Annual Returns, 1926–2008	
Small Stocks	11.7%
Large Stocks	9.6%
Long-Term Government Bonds	5.7%
Treasury Bills (short-term government bonds)	3.7%
Certificates of Deposit (CDs)	3.1%
Inflation (increase in cost of goods over time)	3.0%

Source: Dimensional Fund Advisors, Santa Monica, California

Hypothetical Value of $1 Invested in 1926 at the End of 2008	
Small Stocks	$9,549
Large Stocks	$2,049
Long-Term Government Bonds	$99
Treasury Bills (short-term government bonds)	$21
Certificates of Deposit (CDs)	$13
Inflation (increase in cost of goods over time)	$12

Source: Dimensional Fund Advisors, Santa Monica, California

Stocks

- Investing in stocks does have the risk of losing money.

- If your stock investments are diversified and you stay with your stock investments over a long period of time, the historic risk of losing money is very small.

Three Keys to Investing

1) Time

- Time has an impact on compounding.

> **Compounding**
> Interest, earning interest, earning interest.

> **Rule of 72**
> 72 divided by the interest is equal to the number of years it takes for the investment to double.

- The more time you have for compounding to work, the more to your advantage.

- No matter how little or much time you have, the best time to start is now!

- As you get closer to retirement, you want less uncertainty, so you should have less in stocks and more in fixed-income investments like bonds or CDs.

SESSION **TWO** 47

- You always know the worth of your CDs, but the value of your stocks may be way down when you need to sell.

2) Asset Allocation

- Asset allocation is often credited as having the greatest single impact on long-term return on investment.

> **Asset Allocation**
> The way your assets are distributed between lending and owning types of investments and their subcategories.

- Stocks are in the owning category, but subcategories would include stocks of small or large companies, or companies that are in certain industries or located in other countries.

> **Mutual Fund**
> A pool of dollars from many investors that are invested by a large investment company in a lot of different companies.

- Mutual funds are a means of diversifying.

3) Diversification

- Diversification is about spreading your risk.

> **Diversification**
> Reducing exposure to risk by distributing investments among different companies or securities.

- Diversification is different than asset allocation.

- You could have your investments allocated between different types of assets (stocks, bonds, CDs, etc.), but if all your stock is in one company, you are not diversified.

- Some mutual funds invest in just a certain sector of the overall market, so the stock part of your investments should probably be in more than one mutual fund.

- Investing in index funds can be a good way of diversifying.

> **Index Funds**
> Mutual funds that are indexed to the entire market or certain segment of it; a computer makes sure the returns mirror what the fund is indexed to.

Activity

Given what we've covered, take a few minutes to write down at least one action step you are going to take in relation to asset allocation or diversification. If you'd like to, share your next step with one or two other people.

Taxes

- Taxes can play a significant role in determining investment returns.

- Use tax-deferred investment vehicles that allow investments to grow in value while not being taxed until you draw on the funds.

  » Employer Tax-Deferred Plans – 401(k), 403(b), 457 government plans

> **Employer Tax-Deferred Plans**
> Plans set up by an employer that allow an employee to deposit pre-tax money into an account that grows tax deferred until the employee takes money out.

- Sometimes the employer matches a percent of what the employee puts in.

- If this type of plan is available, it's almost without exception the best place to put money for later-life purposes.

» Individual Retirement Accounts (IRAs)

Individual Retirement Accounts
Plans that an individual establishes for themselves to gain the benefit of tax deferral while governing how their funds are invested.

- With a traditional IRA, the money contributed is not subject to income tax until it is withdrawn in later life.

- Contributions to a Roth IRA are made with money upon which income tax has already been paid.

- For more information on employer tax-deferred plans and the distinction between traditional and Roth IRAs, visit **www.vanguard.com** and click on "Personal Investors", then "Retirement."

Borrowing Against Retirement

- Don't see retirement savings as a place from which to borrow.

- There are multiple disadvantages and dangers from doing so:

  » Loss of the benefit of compounding during the time the funds are not there.

  » Uncertainty about the future.

    · If you leave your employment, the loan must be repaid in a short period of time.

    · If not repaid, taxes will be due and penalties might be assessed.

The Cost of Delay

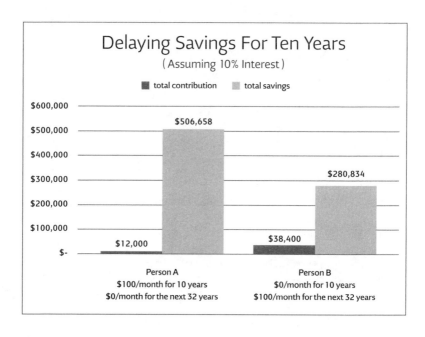

SESSION **TWO**

God's Role

- God's first role is to be our primary source of guidance and wisdom.

  » "The wisdom from above is first pure, then peaceable..." (James 3:17).

  » Engage your financial decisions in prayer and seek trustworthy counsel until you arrive at a decision that is marked by a peacefulness within your spirit.

- God's second role is to be our ultimate source of security — in our later life as well as our present life.

  » We may save up huge amounts of money for later life, but it could all disappear as rust or moths or thieves or economic downturns "break in and steal" (Matthew 6:19).

  » Scripture indicates it is wise to save, but money can never be our ultimate security.

Our Role

- We are to plan and not be like the fool who went to build a tower before calculating the cost (Luke 14:28–30).

- We are to pray.

- We are to "trust in the LORD, and do good" (Psalm 37:3).

Activity

1. What is a specific action step you can take as a result of this workshop?

2. Who can be an accountability partner?

3. *Do you need additional counsel? If so, where will you go to seek it? If you're not sure, how can you find out?*

4. *Are your affairs in order for when later life ends?*

Investments that Last

Let me assume the role of eternal financial counselor and offer this advice:
Choose your investments carefully; compare their returns;
consider their ultimate trustworthiness; and especially compare how they
will be working for you one million years from now.
— RANDY ALCORN

Notes

1   *Webster's Dictionary & Thesaurus, U.S. & World Atlas*, 1997.

2   Some claim the magic age of 65 was guided by German chancellor Bismarck's decision in 1889 to provide governmental support to those who reached that age. At that time, life expectancy was in the mid-40s!

3   Bronte, Lydia, *The Longevity Factor*, New York: HarperCollins, 1993.

4   National Center for Health Statistics, "Health, United States, 2008," http://www.cdc.gov/nchs/data/hus/hus08.pdf.

5   Helman, Ruth, Craig Copeland, and Jack VanDerhei, "*Will More of Us Work Forever? The 2006 Retirement Confidence Survey*," Employee Benefit Research Institute, http://www.ebri.org/pdf/briefspdf/EBRI_IB_04-20061.pdf.

6   Dave, Dhaval, Inas Rashad, and Jasmina Spasojevic, "*The Effects of Retirement on Physical and Mental Health Outcomes*," National Bureau of Economic Research, http://www.nber.org/papers/w12123.

7   Joseph Chamie, former director of the United Nations Population Division, has indicated that developed countries will have to accept a loss of productivity, creativity, and even general economic health if the trend toward retirement at earlier ages continues. (Crossette, Barbara, "Ideas & Trends: Great Expectations; The Retirement Mentality vs. Reality," *The New York Times*, August 15, 1999, section 4, page 1.)

8   Lavelle, Marianne, "7: Work May Add Meaning to Your Later Life," *U.S. News & World Report* 140.22 (June 12, 2006): 58, 60.

Participant's Notes

Participant's Notes

Willow Creek Association
Vision, Training, Resources for Prevailing Churches

This resource was created to serve you and to help you build a local church that prevails. It is just one of many ministry tools published by the Willow Creek Association.

The Willow Creek Association (WCA) was created in 1992 to serve a rapidly growing number of churches from across the denominational spectrum that are committed to helping unchurched people become fully devoted followers of Christ. Membership in the WCA now numbers over 12,000 Member Churches worldwide from more than ninety denominations.

The Willow Creek Association links like-minded Christian leaders with each other and with strategic vision, training and resources in order to help them build prevailing churches designed to reach their redemptive potential.

For specific information about WCA conferences, resources, membership and other ministry services contact:

Willow Creek Association
P.O. Box 3188
Barrington, IL 60011-3188
Phone: 847.570.9812
Fax: 847.765.5046
www.willowcreek.com

Successfully navigate financial challenges and position yourself for lasting success!

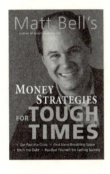

Matt Bell's Money Strategies for Tough Times
Matt Bell
978-1-60006-664-1

Matt Bell's Money Strategies for Tough Times is specially prepared to help you handle (and prevent) the tough times. Practical, proven, sound money strategies, built on the timeless foundation of God's Word, can help you take charge of your financial life.

Learn how to:

- Get out of consumer debt — for good
- Free up money through smarter spending
- Survive unemployment
- Deal with debt collectors and prevent foreclosure
- Choose the best options to pay off debts

To order copies, call NavPress at 1-800-366-7788 or log on to www.navpress.com.